ASk

DG

By Mark Miller

First Edition

Published by

Dinosaur George Media

ISBN: 978-0615939209
Printed in the United States of America

Hi! I'm Dinosaur George.

This is my friend.

He is a *Dyoplosaurus Giganteus*.

You can call him **DG**!

Dyoplosaurus Giganteus

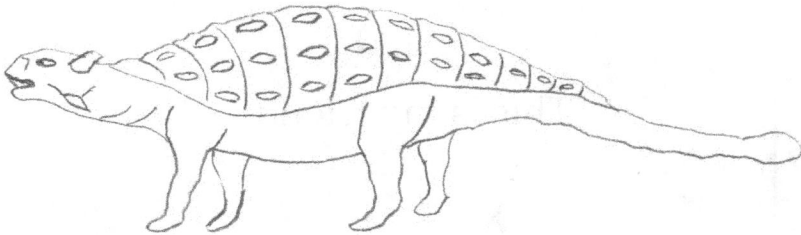

It lived during the Late Cretaceous Period, about 66 to 100 million years ago.

It could grow to about 25 feet long!

It was an herbivore and ate plants like ferns.

You can ask DG anything you want!

My friends all over the world ask lots of interesting questions.

I do my best to answer those questions with the help of my friend, DG.

Are you ready?

Let's go!

Question 1:

Are you a *real* **paleontologist**?

Answer:

I have two answers for that!

First, I will say "no". To me, a real paleontologist is a person that studied in school and earned a degree, or certificate showing they learned a lot. He or she becomes a professor or doctor. That person is the one that becomes a teacher or does research in the field.

But I can also say "yes". I have studied paleontology for over 30 years. I learn new information all the time. I believe I am a link from the hard working professors and doctors to the public and fans like you.

A paleontologist is a person who studies **paleontology**.

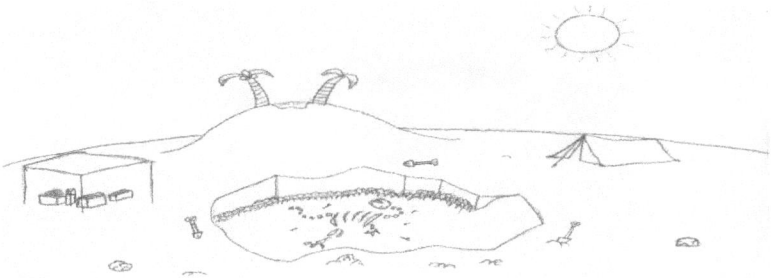

Paleontology: the science that studies animal and plant fossils for information about life in the past.

Question 2:

What is your opinion of the **K-T Boundary**?

Answer:

The K-T Boundary is the geologic marking in the Earth that represents the change from the Mesozoic Era to the Cenozoic Era.

K stands for the Cretaceous period. Funny, Cretaceous doesn't start with a K. The K comes from the German word Kreide, that describes this time period.

T means Tertiary. Scientists changed this to Pg. Pg stands for Paleogene and better describes the era.

Scientists believe that the K-T (or K-Pg) Boundary marks one of the mass extinctions of Earth's history.

An extinction is a rapid or sudden decrease of a certain type of life.

Dinosaurs are extinct.

Most paleontologists believe the K-T Boundary is the time when an asteroid hit the Earth and caused most dinosaurs to become extinct.

Question 3:

What is the most common dinosaur found?

Answer:

The most common dino fossil discovered in North America (and probably the world) is the *Hadrosaur*.

Hadrosaurs were like deer. Imagine ten thousand in a herd roaming across the North American plains.

Hadrosaur

It lived during the Late Cretaceous Period.

It was bipedal. That means it walked on two legs, but it could also walk on all four legs.

What animal do you know that can walk on two legs?

It is the official state dinosaur of New Jersey.

Question 4:

Did the *Stegosaurus* and *Gastonia* need a long time to learn how to use their **defensive weapons?**

Answer:

I believe the answer is *YES*.

Many scientists think that dinosaurs were caring parents. They taught their offspring how to feed and protect themselves.

Young Gastonia had to learn how to use their shoulder spikes for defense from predators.

A predator lives by feeding on its prey.

It is a parent's job to take care of its young.

I think dinosaur parents took care of their babies like your parents take care of you!

Gastonia

It was a type of *Nodosaurid*.

It was an herbivore.

It had defensive spikes on its shoulders and an armored back.

Question 5:

How many teeth did the **Velociraptor** have?

Answer:

That is a scary question!

Velociraptors could have as many as 80 teeth.

How many do you have?

Like a crocodile or shark, Velociraptors could lose teeth and grow new ones.

Once humans lose their baby teeth, they cannot grow new ones to replace their adult teeth.

Velociraptor

It could run as fast as 40 miles per hour.

It was a carnivore. That means it liked to eat meat.

Its name means *Speedy Thief*.

Question 6:

Was the **Short-Faced Bear** the biggest bear ever discovered?

Answer:

The Short-Faced Bear, or *Arctodus*, was the largest bear ever to exist in North America.

There is one other type of bear in the world that may have been bigger. *Ursus Maritimus Tyrannus* was related to modern polar bears.

Because the two types of bears existed at different times, it is hard to say which one was bigger.

Either bear could have reached 15 feet tall, standing on its back legs.

Arctodus (Short-Faced Bear)

It lived between 11 thousand and 800 thousand years ago.

Some of these bears weighed over 2000 pounds.

It might be the largest carnivorous land mammal ever to live in North America.

Question 7:

Did **raptors** tap their toes like they do in Hollywood movies?

Answer:

Unless you are watching a documentary, Hollywood movies are fiction. That means they do not always have to be realistic. Behaviors of dinosaurs in movies are changed to make them scary or exciting.

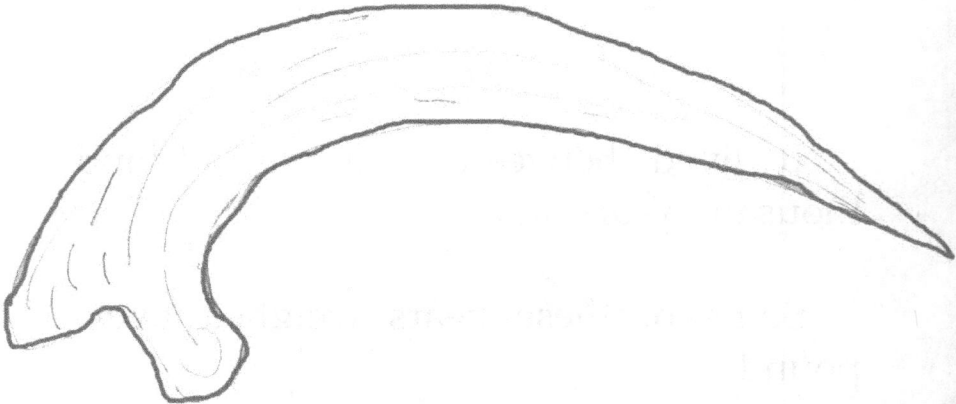

The *Utahraptor* held its large curved claw upright when it walked.

Would a good chef tap his best knife on the floor? No, that would ruin the knife. Do you think a raptor would ruin its best weapon? The raptor needed that claw to stay sharp for hunting.

Utahraptor

First fossil found in the state of Utah in 1975.

At 23 feet long, possibly the biggest of all raptors.

The curved claws on its hind legs grew anywhere from 9 to 12 inches long.

Question 8:

Was **T-Rex** smart enough to trap and contain its food?

Answer:

T-Rex may have had a large brain, but it was not that powerful.

Most likely, the T-Rex hunted by tracking and *ambush*.

Ambush: a surprise attack from a hidden place.

In my opinion, the T-Rex did not have the ability to trap other animals in its territory in order to eat them later.

That would be a lot of work for one T-Rex. Also, the trapped herd would need its own food. The T-Rex could not raise crops like a farmer.

T-Rex (Tyrannosaurus Rex)

T-Rex was not the only tyrannosaur. Members of this family walked on two legs, had tiny arms and a big head with many sharp teeth.

Scientists believe T-Rex could bite with almost 5000 pounds of force. A modern alligator uses about 2000 pounds of force. An average adult human can bite with 175 pounds of force. Talk about power!

T-Rex lived in the Late Cretaceous, about 65 to 70 million years ago.

Question 9:

Who would win in a fight: **Ankylosaurus** or **Triceratops**?

Answer:

I don't think it is very likely that two herbivores would fight each other. If they did, it would likely be about territory or food.

Since no one knows for sure, here is my guess:

The triceratops might say something rude to the ankylosaurus. The triceratops thinks he is a big deal since he has those horns on his head. He has a problem though. His horns are meant for defending against bigger predators. To challenge the ankylosaurus, the triceratops has to get down low.

In this match, I think the ankylosaurus has the advantage. It has an armored back and a low center of gravity. The huge club-like tail is a bonus.

When the triceratops bends low to charge, the ankylosaurus could easily knock it off balance with its strong tail.

Ankylosaurus

Lived in the woodlands of North America.

Boney plates and spikes covered its back.

Its name comes from the ancient Greek word meaning "fused lizard".

Triceratops

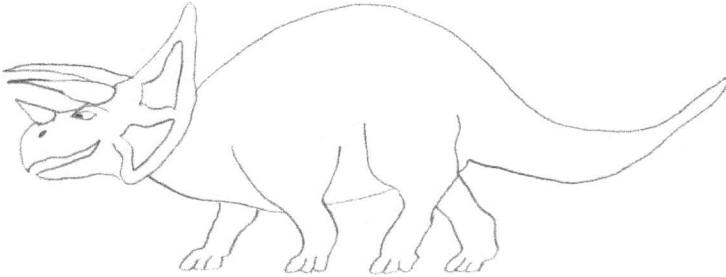

Lived in the late Cretaceous, about 70 million years ago.

Weighed almost 5 tons, about the size of a modern Indian elephant.

One of the last Ceratopsians, or horned dinosaurs, to exist before the K/T Extinction Event.

Question 10:

How did **Ceratopsians** stand?

Answer:

The fun thing about paleontology is that we are always learning something new.

Old information shows the front legs of a ceratopsian out to its side, like a lizard.

Newer information tells us they stood more like a modern rhinoceros.

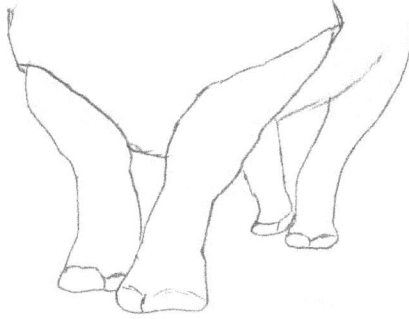

Kelsey, one of the most complete triceratops fossils ever found shows us that the front legs stood somewhere between the old and new information.

With bent legs and toes pointed slightly inward, a ceratopsian probably had great stability and could move faster.

Meet the Paleontologist:

Dinosaur George Blasing is a self-taught paleontologist and animal behaviorist with more than 35 years of study and research. Blasing is a public speaker, writer and television personality who has performed live to over 2 million people and has lectured in over 2800 museums, schools and public events. With the addition of his latest program, Museum in the Classroom, he is now able to bring an entire museum to the schools he visits.

Meet the Author:

Mark currently resides in Florida with his wife and four children. Mark has completed five novels, a screenplay, three digital short story series and several other short stories. The first three books of his *Empyrical Tales* are available in print and eBook. Helping Hands Press published his adaptation of the Christian movie *Daniel's Lot,* a spiritual series called *One,* and a children's educational adventure series called *Small World Global Protection Agency.* Inspirational stories with positive messages are his goal with everything he writes.

Mark believes being a father of four makes him uniquely qualified for young people and adults alike. He hopes his writing sends a positive message with strong role models and a beneficial moral element. His two young daughters unknowingly provided the models that helped create the main character sisters in *The Fourth Queen*.

Meet the Illustrator:

Zak Miller is a high school senior that enjoys spending time with friends and creating his own video games. Zak has been interested in art and computers from a young age. He is currently writing his first novel, a fantasy adventure that spans two universes. He plans to go to college to study computer programming and graphic design.

*Some illustrations are by the author.

Coming Soon!

DINOSAUR GEORGE
AND THE PALEONAUTS

(a middle-grade reader)
Episode One: Raptor Island

To learn more about dinosaurs from
Dinosaur George
please visit his website:

www.DinosaurGeorge.com

To learn more about the author please visit:

www.MillerWords.com

or follow him on Facebook

www.FB.com/MarkMillerAuthor